How the TOILET CHANGED HISTORY

How the
TOILET
CHANGED HISTORY

by Laura Perdew

CONTENT CONSULTANT
Steve Zdatny
Professor of History
University of Vermont

ESSENTIAL LIBRARY OF
INVENTIONS

Essential Library

An Imprint of Abdo Publishing | abdopublishing.com

abdopublishing.com

Published by Abdo Publishing, a division of ABDO, PO Box 398166, Minneapolis, Minnesota 55439. Copyright © 2016 by Abdo Consulting Group, Inc. International copyrights reserved in all countries. No part of this book may be reproduced in any form without written permission from the publisher. Essential Library™ is a trademark and logo of Abdo Publishing.

Printed in the United States of America, North Mankato, Minnesota
052015
092015

Cover Photo: Shutterstock Images (background); Sergiy Tryapitsyn/iStock/Thinkstock, foreground
Interior Photos: Library of Congress, 2, 45; Punch, London, 1849/Universal History Archive/UIG/Bridgeman Images, 6–7; Rsabbatini CC 4.0, 11; Shutterstock Images, 13, 17, 25, 71, 88–89; Photos.com/Thinkstock, 15, 21; Juliane Jacobs/iStock/Thinkstock, 18–19; Joseph Calev/Shutterstock Images, 23; Stefano Du Perac, 27; English School/Private Collection/Bridgeman Images, 28–29; Yuriy Chaban/Hemera/Thinkstock, 30; North Wind Picture Archives, 31; Lucinda Lambton/Arcaid/Corbis, 33; Georgios Kollidas/Shutterstock Images, 35; Hieronymus/Private Collection/© Look and Learn/Elgar Collection/Bridgeman Images, 36–37; Red Line Editorial, 39, 55; Drummond, Samuel/Worshipful Company of Clockmakers' Collection, UK/Bridgeman Images, 41; Public Domain, 42; W. Brown/Otto Herschan/Getty Images, 46–47; Charles Hewitt/Getty Images, 49; Photo Collection Alexander Alland, Sr./Corbis Images, 51; Chicago History Museum/Getty Images, 53; Bettmann/Corbis, 56–57; Bob Brawdy/The Tri-City Herald/AP Images, 61; Szasz-Fabian Jozsef/Shutterstock Images, 63; iStockphoto, 65; AP Images, 66; Ray Tang/REX/Newscom, 67; iStock/Thinkstock, 68–69; Hope Milam/iStock/Thinkstock, 73; Marko Beric/Hemera/Thinkstock, 74; NASA/AP Images, 76; Everett Kennedy Brown/EPA/Newscom, 78–79; BSIP/Newscom, 82; Oleksiy Maksymenko/imageBROKER/Newscom, 83; Mark Boulton/NHPA/Photoshot/Newscom, 85; Zhang Heping/Imaginechina/AP Images, 86; Divyakant Solanki/EPA/Newscom, 95; Deepak Malik/NurPhoto/REX/Newscom, 97; Beth Harpaz/AP Images, 98; Dan Levine/EPA/Newscom, 99

Editor: Megan Anderson
Series Designer: Craig Hinton

Library of Congress Control Number: 2015930962

Cataloging-in-Publication Data

Perdew, Laura.
 How the toilet changed history / Laura Perdew.
  p. cm. -- (Essential library of inventions)
Includes bibliographical references and index.
ISBN 978-1-62403-787-0
1. Toilets--History--Juvenile literature.   2. Inventions--Juvenile literature.
I. Title.
644--dc23

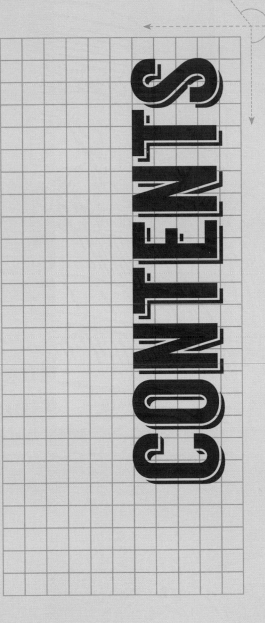

CONTENTS

CHAPTER 1

THE GREAT STINK

In the mid-1800s, cities around the world were growing rapidly. More and more people moved from rural, agricultural areas into urban ones because the cities promised jobs. In London, United Kingdom, for example, the population exploded from approximately 500,000 residents in 1700 to 2.5 million in 1850, making it the largest city in the world at the time.[1] Cities were bustling places and cultural centers. The Industrial Revolution (1760–1840) brought innovations in science, industry, and trade. There were markets, parks, shops, and factories. People were able to

A cartoon from 1849 depicts London's polluted river as "Dirty Father Thames."

enjoy theaters and music halls. Yet for all the advances, in London as well as other urban centers worldwide, there was no means for the safe disposal of human waste.

Watch Your Step and Cover Your Nose

The masses of people living in London in the mid-1800s translated into masses of waste at a time when flushing toilets hadn't yet gained popularity. Some people dumped their waste into cesspits in their cellars, but many of those cesspits leaked or overflowed. Others disposed of human waste by simply throwing it out of windows into the street or defecating directly on the street itself. Either way, the result was that a walk down any city street was downright hazardous.

People called out, "Regardez l'eau!" before tossing their waste out the window, which literally translates to, "Watch out for the water!" This is the origin of the word *loo*, which is what the British call the bathroom.[2]

When it rained, the rainwater cleaned the streets. Waste then went into the various streams and rivers in the city. The rivers, then, acted as sewers, channeling all the waste into London's river Thames. The river also happened to be a significant source of water pumped for human consumption.

During the Victorian era (1837–1901), most people didn't know how to deal with waste. People chucked it out the window, walked around it on the street, and held handkerchiefs over their noses to avoid the smell, but were too polite to discuss it. As a result, sanitation developments were at a standstill in a rapidly growing city.

By the mid-1800s, the Thames was dead. The once-vibrant fishing industry along its banks was gone. Three in 20 babies born in London died before reaching the age of one. In 1848, disease was so rampant in the city it claimed the lives of 14,000 people.[3]

Marginal efforts to clean up London began in September 1848, with the establishment of the Metropolitan Commission of Sewers. Although the government was talking about waste, the efforts were inadequate and did not address the complete overhaul the city's sewage and drainage systems needed.

Snow in London

As the number of people in the city grew, so did the piles of excrement and disease. Even containing it to outhouses did little to curb disease outbreaks because inadequate sewer systems leaked into sources of drinking water. During an 1854 cholera outbreak, Dr. John Snow investigated his theory that the disease spread through infected water. This was a revolutionary idea since most scientists at the time believed the disease spread through the stench in the air,

CHOLERA

The cholera bacteria arrived in London from India in 1831. It is a waterborne disease, transmitted primarily through human feces, and it affects the stomach. As a result, a person infected with cholera experiences great bouts of diarrhea. Not only is this uncomfortable, but one loses great amounts of water at the same time. The water loss quickly affects other organs, including the liver and kidneys. Eventually, fatigue settles in and the patient becomes unconscious. At the time of the London outbreaks, no one knew what caused cholera, nor were there any effective remedies. Two thirds of those who contracted cholera never recovered.[6]

which was known as the miasma theory. People believed they could catch cholera by inhaling air infected by exposure to the disease. Author Steven Johnson explains what Snow proved about cholera:

> Sanitary conditions were crucial to fighting the disease, but foul air had nothing to do with its transmission. Cholera wasn't something you inhaled. It was something you swallowed.[5]

Despite the naysayers, Snow marked on a map all the deaths in one area of London. This revealed deaths were concentrated around a water pump on Broad Street. Snow visited homes and businesses in the area. One remarkable finding was a nearby brewery was unaffected by cholera. Snow believed it was because patrons drank beer, not water.

Confident the water source on Broad Street was contaminated, Snow removed the handle of the pump so no one could use it. The result was a marked drop in deaths in the area, demonstrating a link between cholera and contaminated water. Newly gathered data also revealed death rates were higher in densely populated areas than in rural ones, suggesting the foul urban environment contributed to the disease. During the 1890s, Louis Pasteur's germ theory demonstrated how disease spread and emphasized good hygiene was essential to good health. Despite these discoveries, however, there was no concrete evidence linking contaminated water and disease, and Snow's ideas were dismissed. It took 30 more years until Snow's theory was proven. In the meantime, the miasma theory remained the popular explanation for epidemics.

Summer of 1858

By the summer of 1858, the Thames was an open sewer. Every day, 12 million cubic feet (340,000 cu m) of human waste went into the river.[7] Then, to make

Snow argued there was a misconception about how cholera was spread.

NEW YORK CITY

In the United States, New York City faced a massive influx of immigrants in the 1800s, and the city's sanitation system could not keep up with the increased population. The collection and disposal of human waste became a major issue for city planners. In an attempt to curb the problem, city planners passed regulations directing how people disposed of their waste. This included directions for building and maintaining privies, which were subject to inspection. Finally, in 1871, a new sewer system for the city was approved. Still, rich neighborhoods were connected first, leaving the poor sections of the city with continued waste problems.

matters worse, it was summer and extraordinarily hot and humid in London. The heat, combined with low water levels and accumulated waste, made the smell in London unbearable.

People were so affected by the stench it made the newspapers. The *City Press* in London wrote,

> *Gentility of speech is at an end—[the Thames] stinks; and whoso once inhales the stink can never forget it and can count himself lucky if he lives to remember it.*[8]

Many people even tried soaking linens and curtains in disinfectant and hanging them in windows to combat the smell. But the Great Stink was overpowering. It even kept Parliament from meeting because the Thames flowed right by its windows.

The stench of the River Thames often bothered members of Parliament.

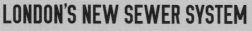

LONDON'S NEW SEWER SYSTEM

When Joseph Bazalgette began the sewer project in London, he faced the challenge of building a system underneath the streets of the world's largest city. Bazalgette began with meticulous designs laying out not only the plans, but also every aspect of the project down to the details of the design of the nuts and bolts to be used. He recruited 22,000 laborers to dig the system by hand using picks and shovels. In total, they removed 3.5 million cubic yards (2.7 million cubic m) of soil. The tunnels themselves were constructed with bricks and cement rather than factory-made pipes. Overall the project took 18 years to complete, disrupting horse-drawn traffic across London and causing some of the world's first traffic jams. But the project, deemed the greatest civil engineering feat of its time, was an enormous success because London's city streets were cleaned up and health improved. More important, the system designed for 2.5 million people is still in operation, serving three times the number of inhabitants.[9]

Yet as disgusting as it was for Londoners, it finally forced the government to take real action. The Metropolitan Board of Works in London was at last given the money and the power to address the problem.

Within a few days, the board appointed Joseph Bazalgette as chief engineer. He designed and oversaw all aspects of the new sewer system in London. His designs included large sewers, fed by smaller, local sewers, which intercepted waste before it reached the Thames. The large sewers collected all waste and deposited it into the Thames east of

Bazalgette's design for London's first sewer system was an engineering achievement.

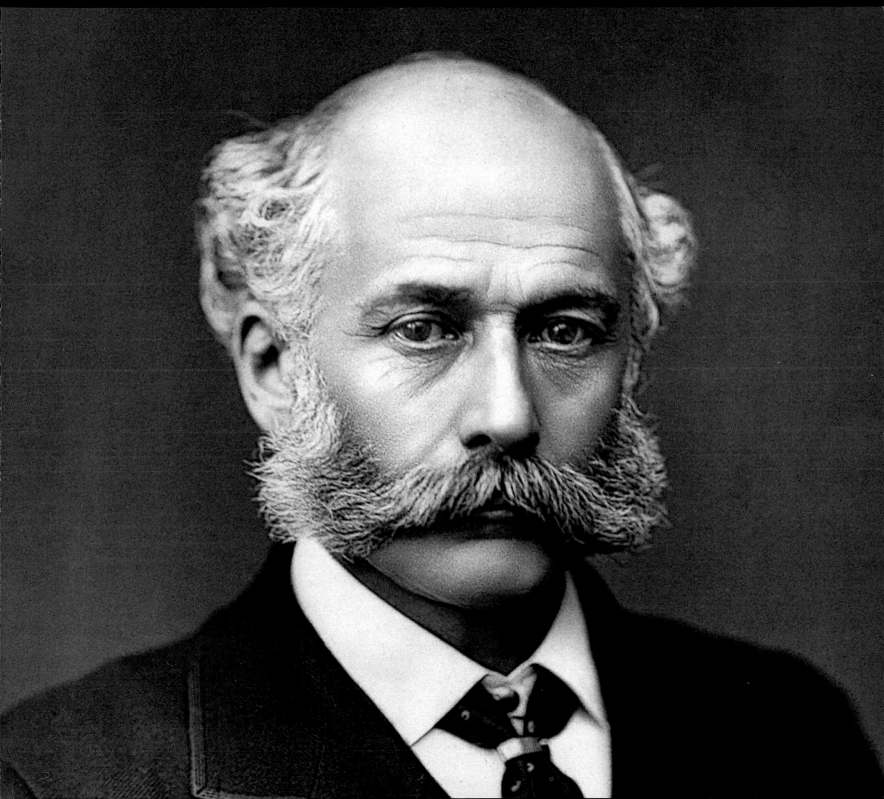

London at high tide; the tide then swept the waste out to sea. At last, waste from cesspits and drains in London was effectively filtered from traveling downriver into the Thames.

Ironically, the sewers were built to remove the smell, which people believed carried the disease. But by removing the sewage, Bazalgette inadvertently ensured drinking water sources were no longer contaminated. By 1865, London had 1,300 miles (2,100 km) of new sewer pipes and a much more pleasant smell. Even more important, public health improved, and cholera died out and never returned to the city.

THE TOILET

3100–2500 BCE
First known toilets appear in the Neolithic site of Skara Brae in modern-day Orkney, Scotland.

300 CE
There are 144 communal latrines and bathhouses in Rome during the height of the Roman Empire.

400s–1600s
Chamber pots, garderobes, and closestools are used as toilets; cesspits and city streets are used for waste disposal.

1592
Sir John Harrington develops a flush toilet for Queen Elizabeth I, but his idea doesn't catch on.

1775
Alexander Cummings invents the first modern flush toilet with a flap at the bottom of the toilet bowl and an S-shaped pipe.

1851
George Jennings introduces the flushing toilet to the masses during the Great Exhibition of the Crystal Palace in London.

Summer 1858
The Great Stink occurs in London.

1972
Congress passes the Clean Water Act to clean up US water by regulating both sewage and chemical waste from industry pumped into waterways.

1988
Congress passes the Ocean Dumping Ban Act to protect the oceans and marine life by prohibiting the dumping of sewage sludge in the oceans.

1990
The Americans with Disabilities Act creates guidelines for making public restrooms accessible to those with disabilities.

1992
The Energy Policy Act of 1992 requires new toilets use only 1.5 gallons (6 L) per flush, as opposed to 3.5 gallons (13 L) per flush.

2000
The United Nations (UN) adopts the Millennium Development Goals, which include improving access to sanitation and clean water worldwide.

2001
The nonprofit World Toilet Organization is founded to improve global sanitation conditions.

2013
A UN resolution sets aside November 19 every year as World Toilet Day.

2014
Approximately 2.5 billion people across the world are still without flush toilets.

CHAPTER 2

ANCIENT TOILETS

All animals, humans or otherwise, produce waste. What goes in must go out. It is a biological necessity that cannot be ignored. Nomadic people did not have problems with waste disposal. Just as a bear does its business in the woods and moves on, nomadic people did as well. The problem with accumulating waste began when people started settling down and grew as the number of people living closely together increased.

Toilets of Ancient Peoples

Attempts to address human waste disposal date back to ancient civilizations. The first known stone toilets were discovered in

The Neolithic site of Skara Brae contains the first evidence of toilets.

NO GREAT STINK IN THE ANCIENT WORLD

Thousands of years before the Great Stink in London in 1858, ancient people understood the connection between filth and disease. While they were not aware of germs and microorganisms, they nonetheless understood clean water and clean streets kept people healthier. Even the Hebrew Bible mentions keeping camps clean. Moses instructed people to set aside areas outside of camps. He told people to dig holes to be used as toilets and to use dirt to cover the waste, thus keeping people and waste apart.

Skara Brae, a Neolithic site in what is now Orkney, Scotland, from approximately 3100 to 2500 BCE.[1]

Mesopotamia is known as the "cradle of civilization," yet perhaps one of the reasons for its success and influence in the world is its people were among the first to tackle human waste issues. Sargon I (1920–1881 BC), a Mesopotamian king, built six privies in his palace. These privies had a place for one to sit comfortably over a cesspit instead of squatting. The seat was much like today's horseshoe design.

The Egyptians likewise had sitting toilets by 2500 BCE. These toilets were flushed manually, using buckets of water dumped into them. The toilets then drained into clay pipes, some of which are still in use today.

In the Indus Valley, there is evidence individual homes were even connected to underground street drains in the third millennium BCE. Baths and privies emptied into these drains, which were connected to cesspits. The pits were then covered to help alleviate the smell.

Sargon I saw the value of having privies in his palace to handle waste.

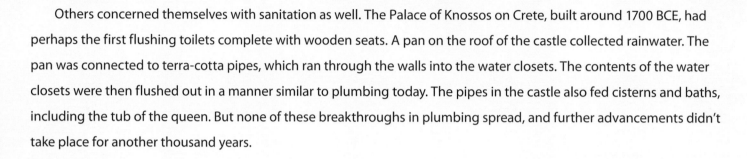

Others concerned themselves with sanitation as well. The Palace of Knossos on Crete, built around 1700 BCE, had perhaps the first flushing toilets complete with wooden seats. A pan on the roof of the castle collected rainwater. The pan was connected to terra-cotta pipes, which ran through the walls into the water closets. The contents of the water closets were then flushed out in a manner similar to plumbing today. The pipes in the castle also fed cisterns and baths, including the tub of the queen. But none of these breakthroughs in plumbing spread, and further advancements didn't take place for another thousand years.

The Romans

The ancient Romans are known for their public bathhouses, hygiene, and sewers. Across the empire, there is evidence of bathhouses and the aqueducts that fed them. Romans tapped into water sources as far as 57 miles (92 km) away and let gravity bring water into their cities via aqueducts.[2] Inside the city, water was collected in cisterns. In the bathhouses, Romans not only bathed together, they also defecated communally. They were gathering places for those who could afford to pay a small fee. Citizens could socialize and conduct business while also "conducting business." By 300 CE, there were 144 communal latrines and

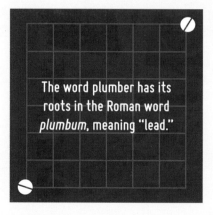

The word plumber has its roots in the Roman word *plumbum*, meaning "lead."

Early Roman toilets, such as these in Ostia Antica, Italy, had a horseshoe shape similar to modern toilets.

bathhouses. One communal latrine, at the Baths of Antonius in Carthage, is said to have had 1,600 marble toilet seats.[3] Many of these buildings were also lavishly decorated with carvings, mosaics, and paintings of gods and goddesses.

The latrines themselves looked like long stone benches, with holes carved out every few feet. The seats were carved above channels through which water flowed from the cisterns. The matter deposited into the channel was then washed out into a great sewer system.

ROMAN TOILET PAPER

The Romans didn't actually have toilet paper at all. But they still needed a way to clean themselves after defecating. Their solution was a long wooden stick wrapped with a sponge. In the communal latrines, a small channel of clean water ran in front of the seats. Users soaked the stick with the sponge in this water and used it to wipe themselves through the latrine holes. Afterward, the stick was left in saltwater until its next use.[4]

Credit for starting the sewer system in Rome goes to the Etruscans. The Etruscans settled in what is now central Italy in the 600s BCE and were eventually assimilated into the Roman Empire. Their greatest contribution was the most significant sewer system in ancient times, called the *Cloaca Maxima, or* "largest sewer." The system was constructed using slave labor. Seven branches of sewers traveled under Rome's streets and connected to the main channel, the Cloaca Maxima, which was 16 feet (5 m) wide and emptied into the Tiber River. The Romans later expanded the system. Today, the Cloaca Maxima connects to Rome's main sewer, 2,500 years after its construction.

Not all Romans, however, could afford to use the communal latrines. Those who could not pay the fee used chamber pots. The pots were simple clay pots that collected fecal matter and urine. After use, they were dumped into public cesspits or sometimes right out the window. In 97 CE, Roman official Sextus Julius Frontinus confronted the issue of polluted streets. He was Rome's water commissioner, and he created laws to forbid waste from being dumped into public water supplies. Those who broke the law were subject to a hefty fine. Frontinus also

Pont du Gard, one of the ancient Roman aqueducts, is located near Nimes, France.

QANATS

In the first millennium BCE, the Persians built water systems called *qanats*. The tunnels ran for many miles, using gravity to bring water into walled cities. Each was dug by hand by slaves and was no wider than a person. Vertical shafts were also dug every 25 yards (23 m) to provide ventilation. These qanats allowed for the irrigation of crops, as well as the collection of water for drinking. In time this engineering technology spread across the East and into the Mediterranean. There are villages in North Africa where water is still delivered via these ancient qanats.

documented the city's waste policies in a pamphlet titled *On the Water-Management of the City of Rome*. Sewers were responsible for improving the smell in Rome.

Ancient Rome was a model for modern sanitation. Engineering advances of this and earlier ancient civilizations allowed for waste to be efficiently washed out of cities through underground channels or pipes. Despite the enormous public health benefits, the evolution and engineering of sanitation came to a standstill when the Roman empire collapsed in 476 CE. But the aqueducts were very well constructed, and some still exist even today.

The Baths of Diocletian were built in 306 CE.

CHAPTER 3

THE COLLAPSE OF
SANITATION

By the 500s CE, the Roman Empire had collapsed. Conquering groups decimated Roman cities and their populations. The toilet and sanitation advances made by the Romans and earlier ancient civilizations were all but forgotten. Thus the Middle Ages became a dark and disgusting time in terms of human waste disposal, one marked by overflowing cesspits, closestools, chamber pots, and piles of human waste on city streets.

Rejecting Roman Ideas

While Romans believed in cleanliness and enjoyed elaborate bathhouses, early Christians promptly dismissed this idea. In fact,

During the Middle Ages, it was common to throw waste out of windows.

they believed in focusing on the spirit and felt the body was a vessel of sin. Cleanliness, to them, meant a sinful display of materialism. Roman baths became associated with wild parties and sin. Because of this, Saint Benedict proclaimed, "to those that are well, and especially for the young, bathing shall seldom be permitted."[1] The result was people in the Middle Ages rarely bathed. But they still ate and drank, so they still had to urinate and defecate. But to further reject Roman mores, Christianity made these natural body functions taboo. They likewise dictated pooping should be done in private, giving rise to the word *privy*, which means "to set apart" in Latin. Thus, instead of getting together as the Romans did, Christians had to find places to go where others wouldn't see them.

One of the most common forms of waste disposal was squatting over a cesspit or into a chamber pot. The problem with the cesspits was that they smelled awful. They often overflowed. In addition, seepage from the cesspits frequently went into the drinking water sources. Chamber pots were no better.

Tossing chamber pot waste out of windows contributed to the stench associated with the Middle Ages.

This illustration from 1630 depicts townspeople trying to escape the Black Death in England.

They needed to be emptied daily to remove the stink from a household. One method of disposal was emptying the pots into the public cesspits or cesspits dug into a home's cellar. Yet other people stayed true to the age-old tradition of flinging the chamber pot's contents out the window onto the street below. There were laws regarding cesspits, but they failed to bring modern hygiene standards. Consequently, the Middle Ages stank.

The other result of poor human waste disposal was the spread of disease and epidemics. In the mid-1300s, a plague known as the Black Death swept across Europe. Fleas infected rats, which spread the disease. Poor sanitation and trash in the streets allowed these pests to flourish. All told, one-third of Europeans died during these outbreaks.[2] In France in 1539, conditions had worsened to the point Francois I, the king, proclaimed he,

The dung pile outside Paris's city walls during the Middle Ages grew so large the wall had to be made taller so invaders couldn't climb the dung pile to attack the city.

Makes known to all present and all to come our displeasure at the considerable deterioration visited upon our good city of Paris and its surroundings, which has in a great many places so degenerated into ruin and destruction that one cannot journey through it either by carriage or on horseback without meeting with great peril or inconvenience.[3]

Garderobes and Closestools

Another toilet system emerged during the Middle Ages. More and more public halls and castles were built with a garderobe integrated into the architecture. The word *garderobe* comes from the French, and originally referred to a small room to put clothes in. But instead of holding clothes, garderobes came to mean small toilet rooms protruding from the side of a building. Inside the garderobe was a small seat with an opening on which to sit and do business. Below the seat was an opening or chute that emptied the contents directly out of the building, usually into a river, moat, or cesspit below it. However, the waste accumulated in the waterways, further spreading disease and increasing stench. It also caused some rivers to stagnate. In London, the Fleet River, which flowed into the river Thames, simply stopped flowing and made the smell unbearable. The Thames was hardly better off in the mid-1300s, as the public latrines dumped 2,000 short tons (1,800 metric tons) of human waste into the river every year.[4] On hot summer days, Parliament members, who met in a building on the banks of the Thames, had to hang scented sheets in the windows to combat the stench, foreshadowing the Great Stink of 1858.

Garderobes sticking out of the sides of a castle would empty into cesspits or rivers outside.

CASTLE MOATS

Moats were built around castles as a means of defense. But what prevented invaders from crossing the moat? Not alligators. Poop. Garderobes built into castles allowed for human waste to fall directly into the moat below. The moats thus served as a cesspit, collecting and fermenting untold amounts of excrement. It was very rare that moats were cleaned and the feces carted away. Invading a castle via moat, therefore, became quite hazardous, not to mention disgusting.

For the wealthier inhabitants in Europe, toilets called closestools also became popular toward the end of the Middle Ages. They consisted of a chair or box with a hole cut in the seat. Below the hole was a pot made of metal or porcelain to collect one's deposit. These needed to be emptied, but the wealthy had servants and maids to do this dirty work.

Other dirty work necessary at the time was the collection of human waste from streets and cesspits. During the Middle Ages, workers called night men scavenged the streets and removed human waste. In homes with cesspits in the cellars, men came in with buckets to empty the pits and remove the waste. While certainly performing a disgusting job, these men were paid well by homeowners. The waste was sold to farmers to use as fertilizer and came to be known as nightsoil.[5]

Sanitation Law

To combat filth and disease, leaders across Europe attempted to enact laws directing the disposal of human waste. In London, for example, the first-ever building code enacted had to do with cesspits. In 1189, the mayor of London set forth the exact measurements of cesspits, their construction, and the materials with which they should be built. Surely this measure helped some, but the pits still needed to be emptied. Otherwise the overflow was revolting. In 1531, Henry VIII issued the first Bill of Sewers in London to appoint officials to inspect drains and sewers. But the danger of bacteria caused by fecal matter in the local water was unknown at the time, and the problems persisted into the 1800s. Even during a bout of cholera, citizens were not interested in paying higher taxes in exchange for a new sewer system.

> Until 1739, men and women did not have separate toilets or privies. The first was at a Paris dance party and read "Men Toilet" and "Women Toilet."[6]

Nearby, in France, lawmakers attempted to curb the problems by issuing orders about the installation of drains in latrines. Orders were issued in 1522, 1525, and in 1539. But, in general, the French seemingly had similar attitudes about the filth as their British counterparts.

Thus while some advances in toilets were made for the wealthier inhabitants of Europe during and after the Middle Ages, the disposal of human waste became a greater and greater issue. Most people didn't have a toilet of any kind. Cesspits and sewers were entirely inadequate, often leading to water contamination. Poop was a problem.

Under Henry VIII's Bill of Sewers, commissioners collected a fee and maintained sewers in their area, which were often open ditches.

CHAPTER 4

FLUSHING GAINS
POPULARITY

Even though the mindset of most people living in the Middle Ages and into the Renaissance was to simply step around the problem of piling poop, not everyone could ignore it. People began to complain of neighbors dumping waste on their property. Others sued when hit with excrement flung out of windows from chamber pots. Even Henry VIII complained, noting the filth and stench in Cambridge. He even blamed health problems on accumulating waste on city streets.

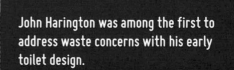

John Harington was among the first to address waste concerns with his early toilet design.

TOILET PAPER

Before the lovely, soft, white roll of conveniently placed toilet paper became available beside most toilets, people used any number of items to clean themselves. The Romans used a sponge on a stick, nobility in England used pages from books, and French royalty used lace. Sailors used the ends of ropes, and others used hay, grass, and newspapers. In the United States, folks commonly used corncobs to do the job. While the first references to toilet paper date back to China in the mid-800s, clearly the rest of the world was not in on the secret. Paper was expensive and valuable. It wasn't until 1857 when American Joseph Gayetty introduced modern toilet paper to the world. His invention was paper medicated with aloe and sold in flat sheets. Still, toilet paper didn't catch on widely until the Scott Company put the paper on rolls in 1890.

Sir John Harington

What little was done about the poop problem was done individually, and usually just for people with means. One individual was Sir John Harington, the godson of Queen Elizabeth I. He designed a mechanical flush toilet for the queen and persuaded her to allow him to install it in her palace in Richmond in 1592.

The innovative device, which Harington named "Ajax," had a cistern of water above the toilet. After using the toilet, users opened a valve to release the water, washing away the contents of the toilet bowl into an underground cesspit. Harington describes the first toilet in his book, *The Metamorphosis of Ajax:*

> *This devise of mine requires not a sea full of water, but a cistern, not a whole Thames full, but halfe a ton full, to keep all sweet and savourie.*[1]

When the user pulls down the handle, it lifts the flush valve chain connected to the flush valve. This allows water to enter the bowl and creates what is called a siphon action. This siphon action forces water and waste to leave the bowl. Then air enters the bowl, which creates the toilet's flushing sound, and stops the siphon action. The supply line then refills the tank with water.

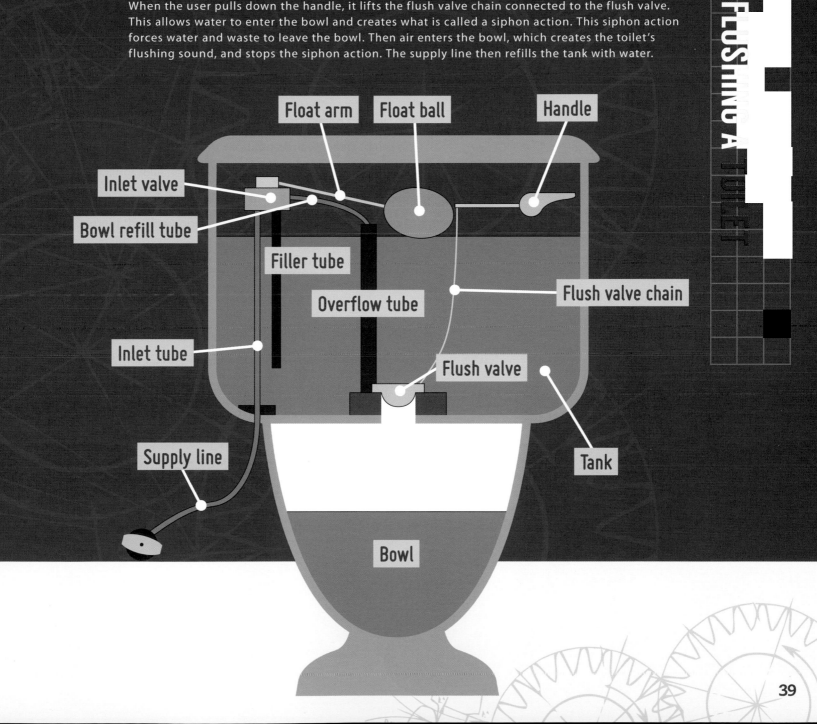

Float arm

Float ball

Handle

Inlet valve

Bowl refill tube

Filler tube

Overflow tube

Flush valve chain

Inlet tube

Flush valve

Supply line

Tank

Bowl

His book includes diagrams, a list of materials needed to build an Ajax, and costs. Yet Harington's design had a critical flaw: smell. While waste was effectively flushed away, it did so through a vertical shaft. So the waste went straight down while the smells from the cesspool were allowed to go straight up. Queen Elizabeth grumbled about the odors, but her godson was never able to solve the problem.

For the most part, Harington's idea failed to catch on. Nevertheless, there is evidence water-run toilets did exist, albeit in small numbers, in England and the rest of Europe. They were called water closets and closely resembled Harington's designs. However, toilets remained low tech for another 200 years: people continued relieving themselves over indoor cesspits and in closestools and chamber pots.

> A board of health was formed in Boston in 1799 to address public health and sanitation issues. American Revolution hero Paul Revere was the board's first president.

The Toilet Evolves

In 1775, British watchmaker Alexander Cummings changed the course of history, forever ridding homes of cesspit fumes and collecting fecal matter. Cummings invented a toilet with a sliding valve at the bottom of a bowl. Pulling a handle attached to a string moved the valve, allowing water to rush in and then out of the bowl. Then the valve moved back into place after the contents were emptied and standing water sealed the bowl. Even more important,

Cummings's toilet had an S-shaped bend in the pipes below the bowl. Once water flushed from the bowl, some remained trapped in the S. The result, then, was that the waste flushed out, but the water in the S kept fumes from traveling back up the pipes into one's home. Cummings was issued the first patent ever for a flushing toilet.

Other inventors improved on Cummings's design. In 1778, another patent was issued, this time to British craftsman Joseph Bramah. Bramah was a cabinetmaker by trade, but with the growing popularity of water closets, he also began installing toilets. Seeking to improve the original sliding valve closure, Bramah came up with a hinged valve to replace Cummings's valve. The new design allowed for contents to empty from the bowl as before, then

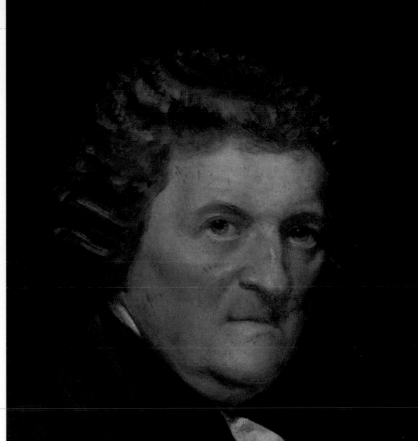

Cummings's S-shaped pipe helped eliminate odor issues.

Crapper's improvements to Cummings's design made the toilet more efficient.

the hinged flap sealed the bowl from the opening. This helped prevent freezing in cold weather. Over the next 11 years, Bramah installed approximately 6,000 of his hinged toilets.[2]

Contrary to urban legend, Thomas Crapper did not invent the toilet. He did, however, make improvements to it. Crapper invented a pull-chain system in 1861 that rapidly forced water from the cistern or tank into the bowl. With this system, users could pull the chain, and then let go, as opposed to holding a chain until the contents of the bowl emptied. Additionally, Crapper's toilet had an airtight seal at the floor. He also patented systems for venting cesspit sewer gas out of buildings. Eventually, Crapper teamed up with pottery maker Thomas Twyford. Twyford made the toilet bowls, and Crapper made the mechanical parts.

The Royal Flush

Despite these advances in toilet technology in the late 1700s, toilets did not go mainstream right away. English engineer and plumber George Jennings found a way to introduce the toilet to the world in 1851. During the construction of London's Crystal Palace, Jennings spoke with Prince Albert and the Royal Commissioners. He proposed building toilets at no cost to the public, essentially creating public restrooms. During the Great Exhibition of the palace, the public saw the benefits of the flush toilet for the first time. Visitors were allowed the opportunity to use the water closets for one penny. Over the next several

American inventor Benjamin Franklin designed the first second-story privy for his home in Philadelphia, where the drains for the upper floor were just above the lower floor privy. This arrangement is still used today.

THE CRAPPER

While Crapper did not invent the toilet, his name is often used as a slang word for the invention. This started during World War I (1914—1918). During the war, American soldiers stationed in Europe discovered the toilets that were common on the other side of the Atlantic. At the time, most of the toilets were made by Thomas Crapper & Company, and thus bore Crapper's logo. When in need of one of Crapper's inventions, men often said, "I'm going to the Crapper." Evidently the word stuck, and they brought it back to the United States with them. Use of the word *crap* can actually be traced back to an 1801 J. Churchill poem about a soldier who receives nature's call.[3]

EXCAVATIONS OF PRIVIES IN NEW YORK CITY

While not the most glamorous form of archaeology, excavating privies is one way to learn how people lived. An excavation of toilet pits in a section of tenements in New York City from the mid to late 1800s revealed the diet of its users. As it turns out, middle-class New Yorkers ate a lot of fish, beef, and potatoes, most likely in the form of stews. These citizens also ate a lot of fruit, pickles from England, and olives from France.

decades, Jennings's public water closets became available in public places around the world.

Americans, on the other hand, often rejected innovations from across the Atlantic Ocean. While some used chamber pots in times of bad weather or illness, most Americans used an outhouse. Outhouses were small, usually wooden buildings erected over a pit, with a pipe leading to the roof for ventilation. Inside the outhouse, users sat on a bench with a hole in it. Some outhouses had just one seat available, but others had two seats or more. While Europe was flushing with great zeal, flush toilets did not become popular in the United States until the mid-1900s.

As new, modern toilets became more and more popular, they were connected to outdated and failing sewer systems. This became a problem not only in London but around the world.

Americans continued using outhouses even as toilets grew in popularity in Europe.

CHAPTER 5

SEWER
SYSTEMS

A t last, in the late 1800s, the popularity of flush toilets grew in Europe. People began installing them in their homes and businesses, and public flushing toilets became available in many places. Toilets were modern and convenient. Although getting rid of waste made homes cleaner, city streets and waterways were not. City planners across the globe were faced with the challenge of how to update sewers below the streets of thriving metropolises.

Joseph Bazalgette and his team oversaw construction of the new London sewer system.

New Systems

More and more people had water piped into their homes toward the end of the 1800s. Yet the water that went in also needed a place to go when it left homes. At first engineers connected drainpipes to the open cesspits. But the open cesspits overflowed regularly and also seeped into water supplies. Rivers and streams were likewise contaminated. Cities across Europe and the United States had a stink similar to the one in London in 1858. Of the situation, a doctor in England said,

> *For the first time in the history of man, the sewage of nearly 3 millions of people had been brought to seethe and ferment under a burning sun, in one vast open cloaca lying in their midst. . . . Stench so foul we may believe had never before ascended to pollute this lower air; never before, at least, had a stink risen to the height of an historic event.*[1]

Not only was the smell unbearable but diseases were rampant, driving the need for updated sewer systems. Engineers began to design and install closed sewer systems, like the one Joseph Bazalgette designed in London. As in other cities, this was an enormous undertaking. Buildings and streets were already in place. Millions of people lived in the cities. Bazalgette was seemingly undaunted by this undertaking, even referring to his

> Today, some US cities hold races to remember their outhouse heritage. Decorated outhouses, with someone sitting inside, are pushed, pulled, or dragged around a racecourse in competition with other racers.

A sewage worker inspects a tunnel under London.

EXPLODING SEWERS

Plumbing during the Victorian era was an extremely dangerous job. The combination of enclosed spaces and the buildup of methane gas in cesspits increased the danger of explosions. The most significant cause of this was poor design, as well as a lack of ventilation. Plumbers came to rely on rats for information when investigating blockages or other problems. If rats scurried around, it meant the sewer was free of gas. But if the rats were dead, it meant one small spark could lead to an explosion.

plan as "simple" in theory.[2] However, Bazalgette also noted sometimes weeks were invested in drawing plans, only to discover a canal or rail line in the way. In such cases, he had to start over again.

HIGH TIDE IN SEATTLE

When the West Coast city of Seattle, Washington, was first founded, it was settled below sea level. Not surprisingly, as the city grew larger, problems with flooding streets increased. In addition, those who had their latrines built over the river were subject to the tides in Puget Sound. Indeed, there are accounts of toilets erupting water three feet (0.9 m) into the air. In order to solve the problems of flooding, as well as exploding toilets, the city streets of Seattle were raised in the 1890s, leaving building entrances two floors below ground. In addition, a retaining wall of stone was erected and backfilled.

US cities reported health and sanitation issues similar to London's. In Chicago, Illinois, for example, 6 percent of the city's residents died from cholera in 1854. One article in the *Chicago Daily Tribune* reported the problem of human waste to be so awful the streets "are ankle deep in festering corruption and rottenness."[3] Yet in order to build underground sewers, the city had to be raised since it already sat at the same level as Lake Michigan. If workers were to dig below that level, the sewers would flood. Buildings were raised an average of 6 feet (1.8 meters), using enormous jacks, and the new sewer system was built.

In Boston, Massachusetts, prior to the mid-1800s, sewer systems were piecemeal, and the drainage system was also inadequate. The city finally addressed the problem in 1875, and Boston's Main Drainage System was designed. Construction of the system took place between 1877 and 1884. It remains the backbone of Boston's modern sewers.

Sewer openings like this one in New York City's East River became more and more common.

The designs in London, Chicago, Boston, and elsewhere included underground tunnels and pipes that used water to move waste along. But the question was, move it where? Experts disagreed on the answer to this question. Some believed human waste should be pumped to agricultural land and used as fertilizer. Others thought the excrement should be pumped directly into nearby water, such as lakes, rivers, or oceans. The belief was, "The solution to pollution is dilution," and over time the water would cleanse itself.[4] This became the prevailing practice, and by 1910, the

SEPTIC SYSTEMS

There are rural areas in the United States still not connected to wastewater pipes. These homes and businesses get water piped in, but the waste goes out to an on-site septic system instead of a waste treatment facility. In such cases, wastewater is piped from a home or building to a septic tank. This underground tank allows solid waste to settle at the bottom and begin decomposing. Wastewater then exits the tank through a pipe high in the tank and into a drain field. Here the wastewater enters the soil, which filters out harmful bacteria, viruses, and other material. The sludge at the bottom of the septic tank needs to be pumped out every few years.

common manner of waste disposal was dumping it into bodies of water. The result, in most cities at least, was cleaner streets, more pleasant air, and less disease.

Water Treatment

The streets and air were cleaner, yet waterways were not. Drinking water was again contaminated. New epidemics arose, as did the debate about treating sewage before dumping it versus filtering water before drinking it. The idea of filtering water before drinking it won out, and thus raw sewage continued to be dumped into waterways. Yet as urban populations grew, the waterways couldn't handle the waste. At the turn of the century, the bay in San Francisco, California, became a festering cesspit. Another great stink.

By the early 1900s, health officials recognized the need to treat sewage before dumping it, and treatment plants were built. In these plants, primary treatment separates the solids; some are filtered with a

Rows of sewer openings in Chicago's Sanitary District in 1928

AMERICAN SOCIETY OF SANITARY ENGINEERING

The American Society of Sanitary Engineering (ASSE) has been "Promoting 'Prevention Rather than Cure' since 1906."[5] That year, Henry B. Davis, chief plumbing inspector for Washington, DC, gathered a group of fellow plumbing inspectors. He wanted to form a group to write rules and regulations regarding plumbing and sanitary engineering, and more specifically to advance the science of sanitation for the sake of public health. The idea was cleanliness, especially with respect to plumbing systems, would result in the better overall health of citizens. The ASSE ultimately pushed for a national plumbing code and regulations. It initiated research on the technical aspects of plumbing as well as the advancement of sanitary science and developed professional qualification standards. It continues to be the face of the plumbing industry.

screen while remaining solids sink to the bottom of a tank. Up until 1972 in the United States, this was the only means of treating the water used in most cities, and the remaining sewage water was then sent into a nearby waterway. After 1972, a secondary step was required. This step feeds oxygen to microorganisms in the sewage, which, in turn, break down any biological matter remaining in the wastewater. Drinking water is often chlorinated as well, in order to kill off any residual bacteria.

Yet, the issue of what to do with the material left at the bottom of the treatment tanks remained. As wastewater moves through a treatment plant, it passes through tanks where the remaining solid pollutants sink to the bottom. This byproduct is called sludge, and up until the 1970s it was dumped into the ocean or rivers.

Wastewater goes through a series of tanks once inside a treatment plant. First it is pretreated with a large rake to remove larger objects. Then it enters the primary sedimentation tank. Solids settled at the bottom are pumped out and slow-moving rakes collect scum floating at the top. At the aeration tank, oxygen helps microorganisms break down water contaminants. In the secondary treatment tank microorganisms decompose organic material and absorb nutrients from aerated water. The remaining sludge settles and is pumped out of the wastewater, which enters the chlorine tank. Chlorine and other chemicals are added to disinfect the water.

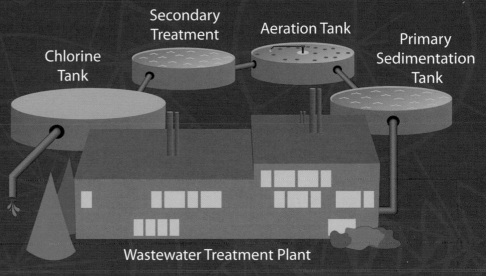

Chlorine Tank

Secondary Treatment

Aeration Tank

Primary Sedimentation Tank

Wastewater Treatment Plant

While toilet technology, sewer systems, and wastewater treatment facilities had improved, human waste was still contaminating waterways. In order to make sure what went down the toilet didn't end up in the wrong place, government action and regulation was needed.

CHAPTER 6

THE POLITICS OF TOILETS

T he new sewer systems and treatment plants built in the early part of the 1900s certainly cleaned up the urban environment and helped to reduce disease. However, the systems were far from perfect. They improved conditions in the cities, relocating the problem to waterways. In 1940, Harold Farnsworth Gray wrote in the *Sewage Works Journal,*

> Urban man today still unnecessarily pollutes streams, bathing beaches, bays and estuaries, without benefit of the excuse of ignorance which was available to his ancestors.[1]

Waste pollution in waterways created environmental hazards, including fires such as this one on the Cuyahoga River in 1969.

HEALTH OF AMERICA'S RIVERS

Despite the advancements in sewage treatment, many US rivers are still polluted, compromising the health of humans and aquatic life. In 2013, the Environmental Protection Agency (EPA) reported more than half of the rivers in the United States are in poor condition. One of the major problems is pollution from phosphorus and nitrogen from wastewater and fertilizer runoff. These nutrients increase algae growth, which competes for oxygen in water needed for plants and fish to survive. Reduced plant growth in turn leads to soil erosion on riverbanks, which leads to flooding. High bacteria levels were also discovered in many streams and rivers.

Gray was among the first to recognize sanitation systems were an environmental concern.

Clean Water Act

It took another 32 years for legislators to take action on what Gray and others already knew: human waste was polluting US waterways. Up to that time, treatment plants simply removed any solids from wastewater before sending it into waterways. The goal had been to improve human health by keeping human waste out of drinking water supplies and off city streets. Further, waste management remained a local concern, not a federal one. So with every flush, liquid sewage kept moving into the nation's water supply. In addition, industrial waste was also dumped into water with little regulation. As a result, *Time* described Ohio's Cuyahoga River in 1969 as "chocolate-brown, oily, bubbling with sub-surface gases."[2] Sewage pollution caused the Cuyahoga to catch fire not once, but twice, that year.

Around the nation, this sewage and other untreated effluent led to low amounts of dissolved oxygen in waterways. In order to support aquatic life, water needs dissolved oxygen. Raw sewage contains organic matter that consumes oxygen. Therefore, the more sewage pumped into the water, the less dissolved oxygen there is for fish and plants. In addition, sewage contains nutrients that are actually present naturally in water and necessary for water plant growth. Yet when excess nutrients are pumped into the water via sewage, there is an overabundance of nutrients, causing overstimulation of water plants. This results in an excessive amount of algae, which in turn blocks sunlight and further chokes fish and plants by competing for oxygen in the water. Finally, as evidenced by outbreaks of cholera and other diseases, untreated sewage contains untold numbers of pathogens that can make it into drinking water sources.

The US Congress passed the Clean Water Act (CWA) of 1972 to clean up the country's water by regulating both sewage and industrial chemical waste pumped into waterways. The CWA's primary objective was to "restore and maintain the chemical, physical and biological integrity of the nation's waters."[3] To do so, thousands of new wastewater treatment plants were built nationwide through federal funding, governed by new regulations for adequate wastewater treatment. This secondary treatment called for by the CWA required organic materials and nutrients polluting waterways to be removed. The preliminary treatment physically removed solid waste, and the secondary treatment treated the water with chemicals.

Ocean Dumping Ban Act

The Clean Water Act was a noble, and even somewhat successful, attempt to clean up polluted waterways. However, the legislation dictated treatment plants must remove additional waste, creating additional sludge. This overabundance of sludge continued to be dumped into the ocean. Scientists eventually discovered what the public flushed down their toilets and cities hauled out to sea affected marine life. While studying ocean dumpsites, scientists found high levels of bacteria and toxins. They also noted shellfish beds were harmed, as well as marine life in the area. In order to protect the oceans, Congress passed the Ocean Dumping Ban Act in 1988.

Still, all that sludge had to go somewhere. The act allowed four years for those who oversaw sewage treatment to devise an alternative plan for getting rid of it. Looking at history, scientists saw the potential of using human waste as fertilizer. New facilities were constructed nationwide, which allowed for further treatment of the sludge. The new process essentially sanitizes wastewater solids to eliminate bacteria generally associated with feces, turning it into a nutrient-rich organic matter. Once the sludge goes through treatment, it is given a new name: biosolids. These biosolids can be safely used as fertilizer to enrich soils and improve crop growth. Cities can also safely burn biosolids or put them in a landfill rather than using them as fertilizer. All methods of disposal are now governed by strict federal and state standards.

Sludge builds up along a storm drain near a pier in Santa Monica, California.

On June 30, 1992, New York became the last city to stop ocean dumping. EPA administrator William K. Reilly said,

The EPA will continue to enforce the consent decrees which require the establishment of long-term, land-based disposal alternatives. We will also continue to encourage solutions that have beneficial uses. Through these efforts, not only are we preventing pollution by protecting the ocean from use as a dump, we are now seeing sludge recognized more and more as a resource, not as a waste.[4]

Energy Policy Act of 1992

If the Ocean Dumping Ban regulated where poop ended up, the Energy Policy Act of 1992 dictated how it got there. Up until the 1990s, toilets used approximately 3.5 gallons (13 L) of water per flush, accounting for approximately half of the water used in a household.[5]

As water conservation movements gained support, the Energy Policy Act of 1992 required all new toilets to use only 1.5 gallons (6 L) per flush. Manufacturers were given two years to comply and redesign toilets and production lines to meet the new specifications. But the rush created flaws, resulting in toilets that clogged easily. Users often had to flush two or three times to wash away waste. And plungers became quite popular.

Designers scrambled to improve efficiency under the new federal regulations. Engineers improved the water channels under the toilet rim in order to increase the velocity of water flushing into a toilet. Other design changes included modified tanks with improved flushing mechanisms and elongated toilet bowls. "It was essentially a change in bowl shape, water flow, and trap design," said Rob Zimmerman, Kohler's Senior

HISTORY OF THE TOILET PLUNGER

With the advent of imperfect low-flow toilets, the toilet plunger became a common household item. The device, a stick with a rubber cup on the end, uses the force of suction to unclog most toilets. Some believe an Englishman named Samuel Prosser first invented the plunger in 1777. But this was before flush toilets were common. Prosser's invention was also more of a device to flush the toilet rather than to unclog it. The invention of the modern plunger is placed between 1850 and 1900, but no patent exists. Other evidence suggests American Jeffrey Gunderson might have invented the plunger in 1932 in the United States.

Pushing a plunger down forces air into the pipe, then pulling it up brings air and water with it, which helps loosen a clog.

63

When low-flush toilets became the only ones on the market following the Energy Policy Act, some Americans smuggled in the old 3.5 gallon- (13 L) per-flush toilets from Canada.

Staff Engineer of Water Conservation Initiatives.[7] American Standard developed one toilet powerful enough to flush 11 golf balls at once.

Thus, by the end of the 1900s, most toilets flushed in the United States did so with only 1.5 gallons (6 L) of water. Once flushed, the sewage drained through complex sewer systems to wastewater treatment facilities regulated by federal policy.

The Energy Policy Act called on manufacturers to redesign toilets to conserve water.

TOILETS
AROUND THE WORLD

From the world's largest restroom to see-through toilets, some very unique and interesting toilets exist in locations throughout the world. The world's largest bathroom is located in Chongqing, China. It is 32,290 square feet (3,000 sq m), four stories tall, and offers 1,000 toilets. The facility opened in 2007 and is located in Chongqing's tourist section. The large site has an Egyptian-style front and offers soothing music. Some of the bathroom's urinals have unique shapes, such as crocodile heads.

The world's largest restroom offers 1,000 toilets and urinals of various shapes and designs.

"We are spreading toilet culture. People can listen to gentle music and watch TV," said tourism official Lu Xiaoqing. "After they use the bathroom they will be very, very happy."[8] One patron said, "Other bathrooms are all the same. This one is very special, I've never seen anything like it."[9]

China is also home to another famous toilet—the solid-gold toilet in Hong Kong. Built in 2001, everything in the restroom is made of gold. The toilet itself is solid 24-karat gold and also coated with gems. The bathroom, designed by Jeweler Lam Sai-wing, is worth more than $29 million. Whenever a patron uses the facility, he or she must wear plastic shoe covers to avoid scuffing the gold bars in the floor.

The experience inside one Basel, Switzerland, toilet might not be for everyone. Located on a street corner, the see-through toilet looks like a mirror on the outside. But when the user enters, the external view is completely transparent. So when in use, a person can see traffic and people passing by the stall.

The "urilift" is another unique urinal, which can be found in various European locations such as Amsterdam, Netherlands. The urilift attempts to discourage nighttime public urination by popping up from below ground at 10 p.m. and disappearing again at 3 a.m. Each unit, which costs approximately $70,000, contains three stalls 6 feet (2 meters) tall and connects directly to the sewer line.

The urilift doesn't offer much privacy, but it discourages public urination.

CHAPTER 7

EXCUSE ME, WHERE'S THE TOILET?

W ith the growing popularity of the flush toilet around the world, many people came to expect to be able to find one just about anywhere. During the 1900s, the toilet began making its appearance in a variety of new places.

Public Restrooms

Public restrooms, in their most basic form, date back to before the Romans and their communal latrines. But it wasn't until the mid-1800s that public restrooms afforded any privacy. In England, the 1848 Public Health Act mandated the construction of Public Necessities in order to combat both disease and smell. Perhaps the

soap

towel

Installation of public restrooms has been mandated in many countries.

PORTABLE TOILETS

Public restrooms are critical in crowded areas or during big events. This need for a portable toilet was first recognized at the shipyards in Long Beach, California, in the 1940s. Workers there had to walk a significant distance to use the bathroom. The solution was a temporary toilet installed closer to the workers. It was made of wood and had a holding tank for waste. Others in the construction industry or those hosting events with large crowds soon recognized the versatility of such an invention. It was self-contained and required no moving parts, power, or water. The heavy wood "cabanas" were replaced with fiberglass models in the early 1970s.[1] By the end of the decade, portable toilets were made using polyethylene, making the toilets lighter, more durable, and easier to clean. Present portable toilets are designed the same way.

first exhibition of public restrooms occurred when George Jennings installed toilets at the Great Exhibition in London in 1851 and charged users a penny for each visit. Not only did this exhibition introduce the public to the flushing toilet, it also highlighted the importance of "private" facilities in public settings for all civilized societies.

Even after all the advances in toilet technology and sewer systems in the modern world, public toilets remain an issue. In large cities there are frequently complaints about the insufficient number of public restrooms. In fact, the number of public restrooms in both New York and London has decreased since 2000. When that happens, people are forced to find somewhere else to relieve themselves. This harkens back to the Middle Ages, when human excrement dotted city streets and alleyways. Public urinals for men called *vespasiennes* were introduced in

People who cannot urinate in public restrooms suffer from paruresis, a social anxiety disorder recognized by the American Psychiatric Association.

Paris, France, in 1841. But these were not very hygienic, so in the 1960s pay toilets with attendants started replacing them. Then, starting in the 1980s, self-cleaning pay toilets called *sanisettes* were installed.

In the early part of the 2000s, New York City also attempted to combat the lack of public restrooms by installing new self-cleaning pay toilets. They were made of steel and glass and cleaned themselves once the user exited. But they never quite worked like they were supposed to. New York has since gone back to installing old-fashioned public restrooms with attendants to clean them.

So called potty parity is another issue facing public restrooms. Lines in women's restrooms are always greater than in men's restrooms. That's because it takes

In Europe, a public toilet is still called "WC" for "water closet."

EVEN SOLDIERS MUST GO

On the battlefield, soldiers often fight without the use of modern plumbing. However, during World War I, they at least understood the basics of sanitation. Hundreds of thousands of soldiers inhabited trenches for years. As a result, innovative servicemen created means to remove human waste. Depending on location and length of stay, "official army business" was dealt with by burning it, burying it, carting it away, or directly disposing of it in a stream or river. Military camps sometimes rely on pit toilets. In such a case, setting up camp includes digging pits. Some are designed simply for squatting over, while others include wood seats upon which to perch. In trenches, soldiers rely on buckets, which can easily be emptied or carried on to the next site.[2]

men half the time to urinate as women. The Potty Parity movement calls attention to the need for more women's stalls than men's in public restrooms. Congress considered this issue in 2010 to address equality in federal buildings, but the Potty Parity Act never passed.

People with disabilities also had to fight for access to public restrooms. Wheelchairs and other devices make accessing small restrooms difficult, if not impossible. Enacted in 1990, the Americans with Disabilities Act (ADA) not only made discrimination against people with disabilities illegal, it also created guidelines for making public restrooms accessible.

Toilets for Travelers

The need for public facilities grew as passenger trains gained popularity in the latter part of the 1800s. For decades, passengers were simply required to wait until the train pulled into the next station or, on longer trips, made a stop for comfort breaks. But as flushable toilets became

Rails and extra space for wheelchairs help people with disabilities use public restrooms.

more popular with the public in their homes, people began to expect them on trains. Soon toilets were located on every train, except those serving only local or urban routes. The toilets on trains were similar to those in homes. But where did the waste go?

Train restrooms can be a tight squeeze for many passengers.

Until the 1980s, waste was simply dumped onto the tracks. In fact, most toilets were simply chutes from the bowl to the bottom of the train, often fitted with a flapper. Passengers could look down the chute to see the tracks rushing by below them. They were also encouraged not to flush while the train was in the station, for obvious reasons. For the most part this kept waste out of the cities, yet nonetheless it posed health risks for rail workers. Since the 1980s, newer trains are designed with waste holding tanks, which frequently include a disinfectant solution. These tanks are emptied between trips. London, however, still has many trains built before the advent of such a system. As a result, even as late as 2014, many stations in London were still served by older train cars, and waste still ended up on the tracks, even in stations.

The toilets in the cramped spaces on airplanes use either a closed waste system or a vacuum waste system. The closed waste system functions similarly to a toilet in a home. The waste is flushed with water into an onboard sewage tank. A vacuum system sucks the waste into the tank using the difference in air pressure inside and outside the plane. When the plane is on the ground, ground crews empty the tanks.

The number of passengers on cruise ships sometimes rivals small cities. And just like small cities, these ships must contend with tens of thousands of gallons of raw sewage per day. Regulations state sewage and other wastewater dumped within 3.5 miles (5.6 km) of the shoreline must be treated, but this is a difficult thing to monitor. Environmental groups argue as the cruise industry has grown, the laws governing waste disposal have not kept up. Vacationers who do not want their waste to pollute the oceans but still want to go on a cruise can look specifically for cruise ships with advanced sewage treatment systems onboard.

CHARLES LINDBERGH

As soon as people began to fly, the need for in-flight "necessities" became a subject of conversation. When Charles Lindbergh successfully completed his transatlantic flight from New York to Paris in 1927, people were curious. King George V asked, "There is one thing I long to know. How did you pee?"[3] Lindbergh described his method. His seat was wicker, with a hole in it. The deposited waste was funneled from the hole into an aluminum can. Then he dumped it over France before landing.

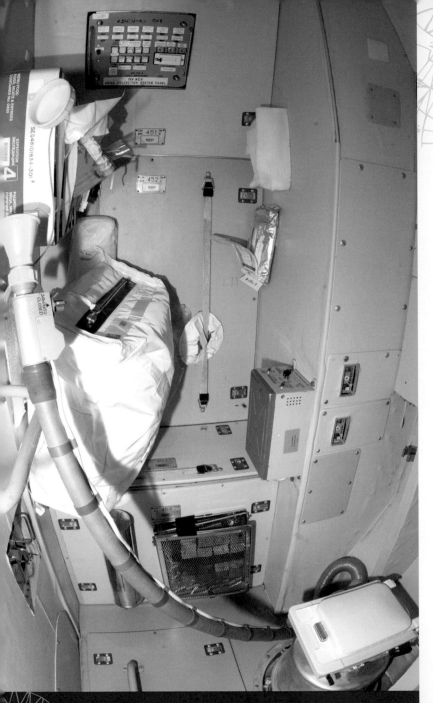

Toilets in space are very different from toilets used on Earth.

Toilets in Space

Imagine having to go to the bathroom without gravity. That is one of the many things astronauts have to learn how to do before being launched into space. They spend a great deal of time toilet training. Astronaut Tom Jones, a veteran who spent a total of 52 days in orbit on four different missions, says everyone gets a laugh at training, but, "You realize that you can't hold it for 18 days. You've got to be able to use the system. And you want to be efficient at it."[4] Training includes a camera under the rim of the toilet, which allows astronauts and their trainers to analyze how the user sits on the toilet. The key is aligning their bodies properly on a toilet and creating a strong seal, or else waste escapes and floats around the spacecraft.

A space toilet itself looks a lot like the ones on earth. The main difference is the vacuum created by the toilet. It ensures a clean separation between the user and his or her deposits. Liquid waste is suctioned into a long tube and stored in the urine container. Solid waste is stored and compressed in the toilet's base. Space toilets have an on switch rather than a flush. When the toilet is switched on, it uses the difference in air pressure to vacuum waste into itself. Urinating is a relatively simply endeavor, with each astronaut, both male and female, having their own custom-shaped funnel. When pooping, astronauts must use their positioning training to properly seat themselves. The toilet also has foot straps and braces that go over the thighs to help the user stay in place in zero gravity.

Astronaut waste does not come back to Earth with them. Urine on the International Space Station is recycled and used as drinking water. Solid waste, on the other hand, gets launched with other trash in capsules, which burn up as they enter Earth's atmosphere.

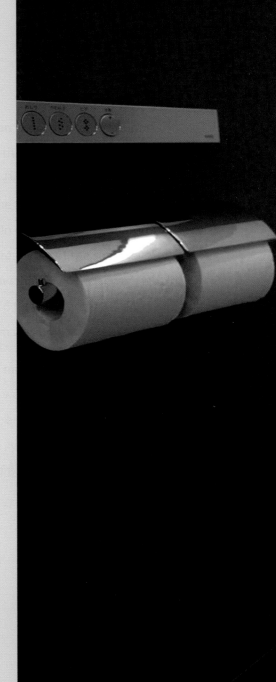

CHAPTER 8

THE MODERN SCIENCE OF TOILETS

For toilet companies to stay competitive, they must stay on the cutting edge of toilet technology. And the engineers behind that science face interdisciplinary challenges. Today's toilet engineers must have an understanding of physics, chemistry, environmental concerns, math, and biology. In addition, water and sanitation issues worldwide are forcing toilet science into new arenas.

The Science of Toilets

American Standard flushed 11 golf balls down a toilet at once to demonstrate the power of one of its low-flush toilets. But golf balls

A TOTO toilet company employee shows off a high-tech toilet in 2005.

TOILET ERGONOMICS

The design of toilets in the Western world has users sitting at a 90-degree angle. But studies have shown squatting is the ergonomically correct method for pooping as it is better for one's health. Sitting upright can lead to diseases in the colon as well as bowel-related illnesses. Nevertheless, in the West, there is a social stigma around squatting to poop. Despite this stigma, a team of designers in the United Kingdom created a toilet ergonomically correct for pooping. The design is a hybrid, combining the desire to sit on a toilet and a place to bring one's legs up to simulate squatting.

are not poop. To determine the efficiency of any toilet design, it must be tested, but using the real thing would be unsanitary. That's where artificial poop comes in. Scientists have spent a significant amount of time developing an artificial poop that closely resembles real human waste in size, weight, water content, and density.

The first company to work with such realistic waste was TOTO in Japan. In fact, the Japanese were using the fake body waste almost 80 years before the American plumbing industry. As a result, TOTO model toilets were ranked first, second, and third in a survey of flush performance in 2002. Not to be outdone, American companies began investing in engineers, research, and design. One of the first challenges was designing a test waste that accurately mimicked the real thing. TOTO's recipe was top secret. The only ingredient they revealed was soybean paste.

Flushing a toilet creates aerosolized bacteria, sending microorganisms onto all the surfaces in the vicinity of the toilet.

By 2003, North American company Maximum Performance created their own recipe using soybean paste, rice, and a sausage machine to create 12-ounce (350 g) fake turds.[1] Thanks to this recipe and hundreds of failed flush tests, American toilet manufacturers have made significant improvements to their toilets.

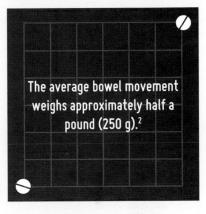

The average bowel movement weighs approximately half a pound (250 g).[2]

But toilet science isn't all about the poop. It also involves understanding physics, specifically fluid dynamics, and applying it to optimize flow in a toilet. Chemistry and materials science applied to clay are also necessary to manufacture the best bowl. Math is applied to developing a good toilet as well. Geometry is an integral part of the engineering design, while statistical analysis allows manufacturers to assess function and reliability. In today's world, toilet design also attempts to address or eliminate water usage. And finally, to make a good toilet, one must have some knowledge of biology and the role of bacteria in toilets and wastewater systems.

High-Tech Toilets

In many countries, dual flush technology handles solid and liquid waste differently. This helps conserve water. But while most people are simply content to have a toilet that flushes properly, the Japanese have continued leading the market in innovative toilet technology. The flush is not enough. As of 2014, the Japanese have developed toilets that

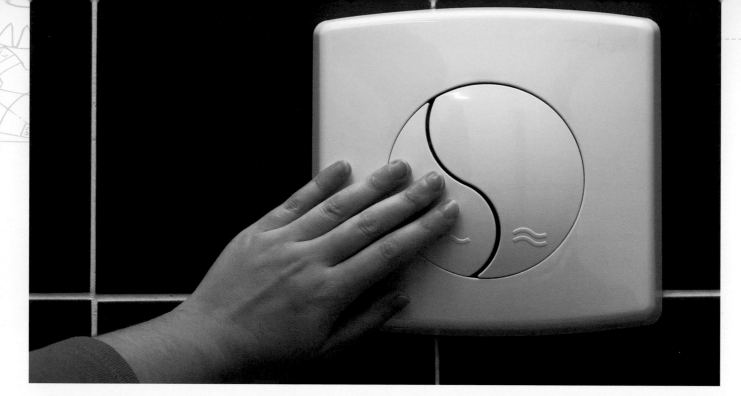

Dual flush technology can help reduce water usage.

can play music, check blood pressure, clean the body, warm the rear, close the seat lid automatically, and even remove undesirable smells from the air. These toilets come with high-tech control panels that can be somewhat daunting for those used to pushing a simple lever and putting the seat down on their own.

Anyone who can navigate the control panel is in for a bathroom treat. First, the seats are not only contoured for comfort but also maintain a user-controlled temperature between 86 and 104 degrees Fahrenheit (30 and 40°C). After business has been conducted, a button-controlled nozzle underneath the seat provides a warm-water cleaning. The nozzle control can also be set to rotate or pulse for the best comfort and cleansing. Once the cleaning is complete, a warm-air dryer allows for hands-free drying. When rested, cleaned, and dried, the user stands. The toilet flushes and automatically closes the lid.

This robo-toilet has a name: the Washlet. Since 1980, more than 20 million Washlets have been sold, and estimates now indicate more people in Japan own a Washlet than a computer.[3] The newest version of the high-tech toilet, the Neorest, takes the Washlet one step further. After being installed in the home, the Neorest toilet takes a couple days to learn its owner's preferences. Once it does, the toilet adjusts the seat and water temperatures accordingly. It also senses when the lid needs to be

A remote control makes the Washlet's high-tech functions even more efficient.

COMPOSTING TOILETS

Another toilet alternative is a composting one. These toilets use the natural process of decomposition to break down human waste without water. Composting toilets look much like toilets in most modern homes. The difference is the waste is not sent to the sewer. Instead, it is collected in a chamber below the toilet. After a deposit, the user adds some kind of organic material, such as sawdust, on top. Then the liquid evaporates and bacteria transforms the remaining solid waste into fertilizer. Done correctly, the resulting compost is safe for handling and using in gardens.

put down. Despite its popularity in Japan, the high-tech toilet has not caught on in the United States.

Biogas

Toilet technology does not have to be flashy to be high tech. Consider toilets that convert human waste into biogas, a fuel that can power lights, stoves, and furnaces. The system involves using organic material to create gas. The organic waste is placed into an airtight tank called a digester. In the tank, microorganisms break down the material into sugar and acids, much like what happens in a human stomach. During this process, gas is created. The gas is processed, distributed, and used as a renewable energy source. The digester also produces solid and liquid material that can be used as fertilizer and compost.

Recycling and reusing human waste solves several problems. First, it keeps raw waste from making its way into waterways. The process also reduces health hazards commonly stemming from fecal matter since pathogens are eliminated in the digester. Solid matter from the digester can be used as fertilizer. In developing countries, indoor

Waste digester units create biogas
in the United Kingdom.

China has taken advantage of the benefits of biogas.

air pollution is an issue because of burning wood used for cooking, especially for women. Cutting wood is also bad for the environment. So the use of biogas as fuel helps address these issues.

In India, the Sulabh International Social Service Organisation has successfully connected public toilets to biogas plants. In order to eliminate the need for handling human waste, the digesters are built underground, and waste flows into them by the force of gravity. China is the nation leading the world in the production of biogas, and the government has supported this endeavor. More than 15 million people in rural China have a biogas digester connected to their toilets. The science behind the system may be technical, but for users there is very little upkeep. One simply needs to use their toilet and then use the free gas produced by the digester.

Turning human waste into a usable gas is just one of the many ways scientists are rethinking the toilet. For all the advances in technology, toilet and sanitation problems persist.

SHOULD YOU HOVER OR COVER?

Many public restrooms provide paper toilet seat covers. And even if they don't, many restroom users choose to line the seat with toilet paper. Others choose to simply hover over the seat. But studies have shown all of these practices are unnecessary. In fact, the average cutting board has 200 times more fecal matter on it than the average toilet seat. It's true. What's worse, the dish sponge sitting next to the sink has 200,000 times more bacteria on it.[5] In the bathroom, if the toilet seat appears clean, it probably is. And, most likely, it is cleaner than other surfaces nearby. The best strategy is proper hand washing when finished.

CHAPTER 9

THE GREAT STINK REVISITED

S ince the days of flinging feces out windows, stepping around waste on sidewalks, and contaminating rivers with human waste, sanitation has come a long way. In the Western world especially, toilets are everywhere, as are clean water and clean streets. But a closer look reveals sanitation still has a long way to go, both in the United States and around the world.

Outdated Infrastructure

While the United States is one of the world's most powerful and wealthy nations, it sits upon outdated and failing pipes and sewage systems. The results include raw sewage backing up into

Proper sanitation is often compromised by aging infrastructure.

INFRASTRUCTURE REPORT CARD

All of America's roads, bridges, transportation systems, power supplies, buildings, and sewer systems make up the nation's infrastructure. The quality of America's infrastructure is graded. Conducted by the American Society of Civil Engineers, the report reveals the condition and performance of the nation's infrastructure. In 2013, America's infrastructure received an overall grade of D+. More specifically, wastewater treatment systems received a D, as did systems providing drinking water to the American public. This suggests a dire need for funds to expand and improve wastewater treatment in America.

people's homes regularly and also flowing into waterways untreated. Untreated sewage ends up in drinking water and waterways and on private property.

The Natural Resources Defense Council and the Environmental Integrity Project released a 2004 report titled "Swimming in Sewage." The report revealed the depth and impact of the problem. Billions of dollars were spent annually to clean up sewage spills and fix leaking or broken pipes. In addition, lost tourism and productivity and increased medical treatment associated with sewer issues cost money. The report likewise predicted the problem would only get worse as populations grow, as storm water collection systems are further stressed by urban sprawl, and as storms grow increasingly severe due to climate change.

Around the World

Despite infrastructure issues in the United States that need to be addressed, most Americans have daily access to proper sanitation.

Yet across the globe, as of 2013, 35 percent of the world's people did not have access to a toilet. That means approximately 2.5 billion people must find an alternative place to relieve themselves. Many, up to 1 billion people, simply practice open defecation.[1]

Because human waste contains communicable diseases, bacteria, viruses, parasites, and worm eggs, people living in areas without toilets are regularly sickened. Diarrhea is one of the most common illnesses, killing approximately 2,200 children per day.[2] That number is greater than those killed by malaria, AIDS, and measles combined. It is the second-largest killer of children in the world. The areas of the world most affected are sub-Saharan Africa and Southern and Eastern Asia.

The costs of not having toilet facilities run even deeper than health issues. A lack of running water also keeps many girls from attending school, especially those reaching puberty. Female students often do not continue their education not only because of privacy issues such as menstruation, but also because they are responsible for collecting water for their families. In India alone, 25 percent of girls drop out of school because of a lack of adequate facilities.[3]

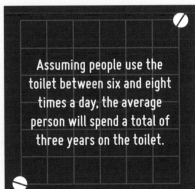

Assuming people use the toilet between six and eight times a day, the average person will spend a total of three years on the toilet.

Lack of toilets is also a safety issue for many women. More than 1 billion women worldwide risk shame, harassment, and attack each time they need to relieve themselves. Many women and girls hold their bladders and bowels throughout the day, waiting for nightfall for some privacy. Even those with access to public toilets must often walk long distances, often in the dark. During these times, women are vulnerable to attacks and rape, especially in areas where women are known to openly defecate and near public facilities. This problem is illustrated by a May 2014 incident in India. Two teen girls from the village of Katra Sahadatganj left their houses to defecate. The girls didn't have toilets in their homes or access to public ones in this remote village, so they waited for nightfall and went together. They never returned home, and their mutilated bodies were found hung from a tree. Protests about this type of ongoing violence and the lack of safe toilets erupted in India.

Toilet Projects

According to the World Toilet Organization, every dollar spent investing in clean water and sanitation will generate a return of eight dollars in increased productivity, reduced health-care costs, and saved time.[4] Toilets also promote safety and dignity for all humans. People are beginning to talk about toilets publicly. The need to urinate and defecate is universal, but discussing the subject of toilets is still avoided in many parts of the world. In order to raise awareness, individuals and organizations across the world have started campaigns. One of the most significant steps toward improving sanitation worldwide occurred in 2000, when the United Nations (UN) adopted the Millennium Development Goals to create a global partnership of world leaders to address extreme poverty. These goals included improving access to sanitation and clean water, moving toilets into the international spotlight for the first time in history.

Among other UN campaigns, World Toilet Day is gaining publicity. Celebrated on November 19 every year, World Toilet Day was adopted by a UN resolution in 2013 in order to raise awareness about the 2.5 billion people who do not have access to proper sanitation. Based on the belief that access to clean water and sanitation is a human right, the objective of World Toilet Day is to make sanitation a global priority. On November 19, people around the world take action, using social media to draw attention to the sanitation issue, breaking the toilet taboo by talking openly about toilets, donating money, and more.

MR. TOILET

Jack Sim has a nickname he is quite proud of: "Mr. Toilet." He is the founder of the World Toilet Organization, and he has worked for decades to educate people and to bring toilets and proper sanitation to those who need it. He is the voice for toilets. "What you don't talk about, you cannot improve," Sim said.[5] Since 2001, he has also hosted the World Toilet Summit, an international event that brings attention to the plight of billions. Sim's work has brought sanitation into global news. He looks forward to the day when everyone on the planet has access to clean toilets at any time, any day.

ARBORLOOS

In east Africa, a new type of toilet is gaining popularity: the arborloo. A nonprofit organization realized the need for toilets in Ethiopia and came up with a simple, inexpensive solution. An arborloo begins with a lined pit 3 feet (0.9 m) deep and 2 feet (0.6 m) wide. Then, a portable concrete slab with a hole in the middle is placed over the pit. Next, walls and a door are constructed over the pit using available materials. A family of five to six can use the pit for about a year, adding soil or other materials after each use to aid composting and prevent smells. Once the pit is full, a new pit is dug, and the slab and arborloo walls are moved over the new pit. The old pit is topped with at least 6 inches (15 cm) of topsoil, and then a tree seedling is planted, in time providing fruit and shade for the family.

Another organization working to provide access to sanitation is the World Toilet Organization (WTO). Founded on November 19, 2001, the WTO is a nonprofit focused on improving global sanitation conditions. The WTO also educates people at the local to global levels, creates corporate partnerships to advance the cause, raises funds, and uses the media to promote awareness.

The Bill and Melinda Gates Foundation addresses sanitation issues as well, through its Water, Sanitation & Hygiene program. The program's goal is "to enable universal access to sustainable sanitation services by supporting the development of radically new sanitation technologies . . . "[6] It focuses primarily on urban areas and the developing world as they seek innovative solutions. One obstacle to universal toilet access in these densely populated areas is the lack of water and proper sewer systems. To address this,

> The first Hollywood movie to feature a toilet flushing was Alfred Hitchcock's *Psycho* in 1960. The first television appearance for the toilet was on the sitcom *Leave It to Beaver* (1957—1963).

An Indian girl brings a bucket to use the latrine in the outskirts of Mumbai, India.

the foundation is developing toilet systems that can operate without sewers. It is also a global advocate for public toilets and new toilet design.

In India, toilet issues are the focus of Dr. Bindeshwar Pathak. He is known as the toilet guru because of his work in this area. Pathak works to break the social taboo around discussing toilets and bodily functions while also providing toilets to poor people. By doing so, he is pushing social change in India, making people aware it is a right and a matter of health to have a toilet. As of 2014, Pathak's organization, Sulabh International, has built 1.3 million toilets in homes

MAHATMA GANDHI

Mahatma Gandhi is best known for his peaceful fight for India's independence in the 1900s. But he also took on another cause—toilets. As a result of India's deep-rooted caste system, the lowliest citizens, the untouchables, were the ones who cleaned out latrines. In 1901, Gandhi proclaimed the practice disgraceful. To bring attention to the issue, he publicly cleaned his own toilet. In addition, Gandhi developed a composting system that did not need to be cleaned out. He dug a pit for himself, and after it was filled he covered it with soil and dug a new one. Decades later, in the 1970s, this model inspired Dr. Pathak, who began to provide toilets for India's poor.

in his country.[7] The group also continues to educate people about the connection between feces and disease.

Individuals such as Dr. Pathak are working to improve sanitation worldwide. He and millions of others have committed themselves to providing dignity and sanitation for all. On World Toilet Day 2014, the deputy secretary-general of the United Nations, Jan Eliasson, released a video message. He declared the plight of billions of people without access to proper sanitation and the ongoing deaths of children from preventable diseases is unacceptable. He wants people worldwide to talk openly about toilets in order to break the silence and bring universal access to adequate sanitation. Eliasson said,

Let us bring the sanitation challenge out of the shadows, face it head on, and work together towards an end to open defecation and substantially better access to sanitation.[8]

Dr. Pathak works to provide sanitary waste disposal to the millions of Indians who need it.

THE NEXT GENERATION: TOILET EVOLUTION

Toilet technology in the future is evolving along two very different tracks, depending on location. In the advanced world, the future toilet is all about comfort and efficiency. High-tech thrones feature sleek tankless designs, seats that close automatically, deodorizers that spray into the room after use, and a touchless flush. Some toilets even analyze aspects of a user's health, such as body temperature, blood sugar, and blood pressure. Many of the new, modern models also warm the seat and play music.

Yet the true technological advancements in toilet technology are taking place in

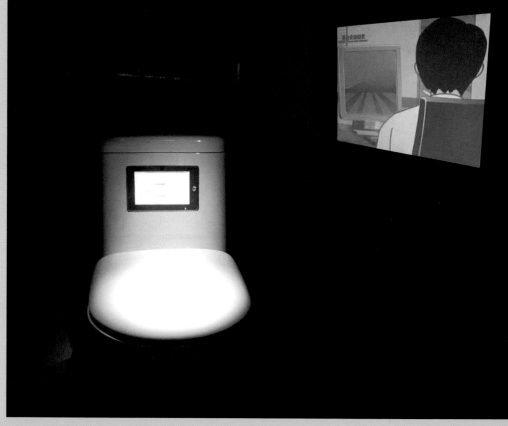

This toilet comes with a digital screen that shows health data collected by analyzing urine.

developing countries. In these countries, new toilets must work without running water, sewers, or electricity. They must also cost very little to run. Toilet technology in developing countries also seeks to capture the energy produced by waste. Individuals and organizations worldwide are designing toilets for the 2.5 billion people who do not have access to proper sanitation.[9]

Since 2011, the Bill and Melinda Gates Foundation has sponsored the Reinvent the Toilet Challenge to promote solutions for safe, inexpensive, and sustainable human waste management. Each year, the Reinvent the Toilet Fair showcases sanitation technology and awards grants to researchers who create innovative designs for reinventing the toilet. Some of the new designs include a solar-powered toilet that uses the sun's energy to break down waste. It dries feces and produces storable hydrogen gas. Another uses a hand crank to grind the feces, which heats the fecal matter and kills most pathogens.

This solar steam sterilizer for human waste was among many sanitation technology designs at the Reinvent the Toilet Fair in 2012.

DATE OF INVENTION

1775

KEY PLAYERS

- The Etruscans develop an elaborate sewer system in Rome, much of which is still in use today.

- Sir John Harington invents one of the first flush toilets in 1592.

- Alexander Cummings invents the modern flush toilet in 1775. It includes a sliding valve covering the bowl and S-pipes.

- Chief engineer Joseph Bazalgette designs a new sewer system in London in 1858.

- India's Dr. Bindeshwar Pathak leads an effort to provide toilets for everyone in his country and spread knowledge about the universal need for sanitation.

KEY TECHNOLOGIES

Use of water in both open and closed sewers became necessary toward the late 1800s to wash away waste. The development of S-pipes helped to prevent waste odors from traveling back up the pipes in previous toilet designs. As toilets became more common, many countries designed improved infrastructure and water treatment facilities with physical, chemical, and biological processes to treat raw sewage. Biogas technology turns human waste into a usable fuel and fertilizer, without the need for water or sewer systems.

EVOLUTION AND UPGRADES

▶ S-shaped pipe, 1775

▶ Hinged valve closure, 1778

▶ Pull-chain system, 1861

▶ Sewer systems, late 1800s

▶ Wastewater treatment, early 1900s

IMPACT ON SOCIETY

The development of the toilet allowed for a healthy, safe, dignified place for people to urinate and defecate. Sewer systems keep filth off of streets, thus cleaning up cities and ending cholera outbreaks. Treatment facilities allow for the safe collection and treatment of raw sewage, thus protecting both human and marine life.

QUOTE

"Urban man today still unnecessarily pollutes streams, bathing beaches, bays and estuaries, without benefit of the excuse of ignorance which was available to his ancestors."

—*Harold Farnsworth Gray*

aerosolize

To convert into a fine spray in the air.

biogas

A gas produced during the decomposition of organic waste, including human feces, which can be used as fuel.

biosolid

The nutrient-rich organic byproduct left behind at a wastewater treatment facility, which can be recycled and used as fertilizer.

cesspit

A hole in the ground designed to hold sewage and trash.

chamber pot

A pot into which one urinates or defecates.

cistern

An underground container used to collect waste.

closestool

A box with a circular opening that emptied into a chamber pot below.

defecate

Passing solid waste from the body.

effluent

Liquid sewage discharged into a body of water.

ergonomics

The science of designing and ordering things so people can use them easily and safely.

feces

Waste discharged from one's body.

fluid dynamics

The study of the movement of liquids and gases.

garderobe

A medieval toilet room built into the wall of a castle, usually overhanging a moat or river.

latrine

A receptacle, such as a pit in the ground, for use as a toilet.

miasmatic theory

The belief diseases are caused by odors in the air.

open defecation

Relieving one's bowels out in the open rather than in a toilet.

patent

A permit issued by a government that grants a person the legal right to use or market an invention, technology, or process.

sludge

The solid byproduct produced during the wastewater treatment process.

water closet

A room that used gravity and water to wash away human waste into a waterway below.

SELECTED BIBLIOGRAPHY

Basset, John. "Great Stink." *YouTube*. YouTube, 15 Feb. 2014. Web. 21 Oct. 2014.

George, Rose. *The Big Necessity: The Unmentionable World of Human Waste and Why It Matters*. New York: Metropolitan, 2008. Print.

Horan, Julie L. *The Porcelain God: A Social History of the Toilet*. Secaucus, NJ: Carol, 1996. Print.

"Sulabh International—Museum of Toilets." *Sulabh International Museum of Toilets*. Sulabh International Museum of Toilets, May 1995. Web. 23 Nov. 2014.

FURTHER READINGS

Albee, Sarah. *Poop Happened! A History of the World from the Bottom Up*. New York: Walker, 2010. Print.

Gregory, Morna E., and Sian James. *Toilets of the World*. London: Merrell, 2006. Print.

MacDonald, Fiona, and David Salariya. *You Wouldn't Want to Live without Toilets*. New York: Scholastic, 2014. Print.

WEBSITES

To learn more about Essential Library of Inventions, visit **booklinks.abdopublishing.com**. These links are routinely monitored and updated to provide the most current information available.

FOR MORE INFORMATION

For more information on this subject, contact or visit the following organizations:

Environmental Protection Agency's Office of Wastewater Management

1200 Pennsylvania Avenue, NW
Washington, DC 20460
800-426-4791
http://water.epa.gov/polwaste/wastewater/index.cfm

This government office oversees the management of the nation's wastewater.

Sulabh International Museum of Toilets

Sulabh Bhawan, Palam Dabri Marg, Mahavir Enclave
Palam, New Delhi, DL 110045
+91-011-2503 1518 & 19
http://www.sulabhtoiletmuseum.org

This museum in India is entirely dedicated to the history of toilets! It includes artifacts and information on toilet technology around the world.

SOURCE NOTES

Chapter 1. The Great Stink

1. John Basset. "Great Stink." *YouTube*. YouTube, 15 Feb. 2014. Web. 16 Apr. 2015.

2. Ibid.

3. Ibid.

4. Julie L. Horan. *The Porcelain God—A Social History of the Toilet*. Secaucus, NJ: Carol, 1996. Print. 79.

5. Steven Johnson. *The Ghost Map: The Story of London's Most Terrifying Epidemic—and How It Changed Science, Cities, and the Modern World*. New York: Riverhead, 2006. Print. 71–72.

6. John Basset. "Great Stink." *YouTube*. YouTube, 15 Feb. 2014. Web. 16 Apr. 2015.

7. NV AtCEPImperial. "The Great Stink." *YouTube*. YouTube, 18 Apr. 2013. Web. 16 Apr. 2015.

8. W. Hodding Carter. *Flushed—How the Plumber Saved Civilization*. New York: Atria, 2006. Print. 99.

9. John Basset. "Great Stink." *YouTube*. YouTube, 15 Feb. 2014. Web. 16 Apr. 2015.

Chapter 2. Ancient Toilets

1. Joshua J. Mark. "Skara Brae." *Ancient History Encyclopedia*. Ancient History Encyclopedia, 18 Oct. 2012. Web. 16 Apr. 2015.

2. "Aqueduct." *Encyclopedia Britannica*. Encyclopedia Britannica, 3 Jan. 2008. Web. 16 Apr. 2015.

3. W. Hodding Carter. *Flushed—How the Plumber Saved Civilization*. New York: Atria, 2006. Print. 33–34.

4. John Basset. "Great Stink." *YouTube*. YouTube, 15 Feb. 2014. Web. 16 Apr. 2015.

Chapter 3. The Collapse of Sanitation

1. "The History of Plumbing." *ThePlumber*. ThePlumber, n.d. Web. 16 Apr. 2015.

2. Julie L. Horan. *The Porcelain God—A Social History of the Toilet*. Secaucus, NJ: Carol, 1996. Print. 21–22.

3. W. Hodding Carter. *Flushed—How the Plumber Saved Civilization*. New York: Atria, 2006. Print. 87–88.

4. Julie L. Horan. *The Porcelain God—A Social History of the Toilet*. Secaucus, NJ: Carol, 1996. Print. 31–32.

5. W. Hodding Carter. *Flushed—How the Plumber Saved Civilization*. New York: Atria, 2006. Print. 90.

6. Lawrence Wright. *Clean and Decent*. Toronto: U of Toronto P, 1967. Print. 103.

Chapter 4. Flushing Gains Popularity

1. Julie L. Horan. *The Porcelain God—A Social History of the Toilet*. Secaucus, NJ: Carol, 1996. Print. 48.

2. W. Hodding Carter. *Flushed—How the Plumber Saved Civilization*. New York: Atria, 2006. Print. 154–155.

3. Maddie Crum. "Word Meaning: The Etymology Of 'Crap.'" *Huffington Post*. Huffington Post, 2 Oct. 2012. Web. 16 Apr. 2015.

Chapter 5. Sewer Systems

1. Joaquin I. Uy. "Cesspools and Cholera: The Development of the Modern Sewer." *Greywater Action*. Greywater Action, n.d. Web. 16 Apr. 2015.

2. John Basset. "Great Stink." *YouTube*. YouTube, 15 Feb. 2014. Web. 16 Apr. 2015.

3. Gayle Soucek. *Carson's: The History of a Chicago Shopping Landmark*. Chicago: History, 2013. Print. 33.

4. "Marine Pollution." *National Geographic*. National Geographic, n.d. Web. 16 Apr. 2015.

5. "ASSE—The Story." *ASSE International*. ASSE International, n.d. Web. 16 Apr. 2015.

SOURCE NOTES CONTINUED

Chapter 6. The Politics of Toilets

1. Joaquin I. Uy. "Cesspools and Cholera: The Development of the Modern Sewer." *Greywater Action*. Greywater Action, n.d. Web. 16 Apr. 2015.

2. Rose George. *The Big Necessity—The Unmentionable World of Human Waste and Why It Matters*. New York: Metropolitan, 2008. Print. 155.

3. *Primer for Municipal Wastewater Treatment Systems*. United States Environmental Protection Agency, Sept. 2004. Web. 16 Apr. 2015.

4. "Reilly in New York to Mark End of Sewage Sludge Dumping." *United States Environmental Protection Agency*. United States Environmental Protection Agency, 30 June 1992. Web. 16 Apr. 2015.

5. Rose George. *The Big Necessity—The Unmentionable World of Human Waste and Why It Matters*. New York: Metropolitan, 2008. Print. 54.

6. "Water Questions & Answers." *USGS*. US Geological Survey, n.d. Web. 16 Apr. 2015.

7. Benjamin Hardy. "Low-Flow Toilets 101." *Bob Vila*. Bobvila.com, n.d. Web. 16 Apr. 2015.

8. "World's Largest Public Restroom Facility Opens." *NBC News*. NBC News, 6 July 2007. Web. 16 Apr. 2015.

9. Ibid.

Chapter 7. Excuse Me, Where's the Toilet?

1. "The History of Portable Toilets." *Diamond Environmental Services*. Diamond Environmental Services, n.d. Web. 16 Apr. 2015.

2. Julie L. Horan. *The Porcelain God—A Social History of the Toilet*. Secaucus, NJ: Carol, 1996. Print. 169–177.

3. Blythe Haaga. "On Transatlantic Bathroom Breaks." *NPR*. NPR, 4 Mar. 2012. Web. 16 Apr. 2015.

4. Paul Bisceglio. "How Do Astronauts Go to the Bathroom in Space?" *Smithsonian.com*. Smithsonian.com, 13 Mar. 2013. Web. 16 Apr. 2015.

108

Chapter 8. The Modern Science of Toilets

1. Michaeleen Doucleff. "Why Is the World's Largest Foundation Buying Fake Poop?" *NPR*. NPR, 10 Aug. 2012. Web. 16 Apr. 2015.

2. Rose George. *The Big Necessity—The Unmentionable World of Human Waste and Why It Matters*. New York: Metropolitan, 2008. Print. 57.

3. Ibid. 41–42.

4. "What is FMT?" *Fecal Transplant Foundation*. Fecal Transplant Foundation, n.d. Web. 16 Apr. 2015.

5. AsapSCIENCE. "Should You Hover or Cover the Toilet Seat?" *YouTube*. YouTube, 16 June 2014. Web. 16 Apr. 2015.

Chapter 9. The Great Stink Revisited

1. Jon Springer. "Why World Toilet Day Should Matter To You." *Forbes*. Forbes, 18 Nov. 2014. Web. 16 Apr. 2015.

2. Ibid.

3. Rose George. "Let's Talk Crap. Seriously." *TED*. TED, Feb. 2013. Web. 16 Apr. 2015.

4. "World Toilet Organization." *World Toilet Organization*. World Toilet Organization, n.d. Web. 16 Apr. 2015.

5. World Toilet Organization. "Meet Mr. Toilet." *YouTube*. YouTube, 21 Sept. 2012. Web. 16 Apr. 2015.

6. "Water, Sanitation & Hygiene." *Bill & Melinda Gates Foundation*. Bill & Melinda Gates Foundation, n.d. Web. 16 Apr. 2015.

7. Julie McCarthy. "How a Lack of Toilets Puts India's Women at Risk of Assault." *NPR*. NPR, 9 June 2014. Web. 16 Apr. 2015.

8. WaterAid. "A Message from the UN Deputy Secretary-General on World Toilet Day 2014." *YouTube*. YouTube, 17 Nov. 2014. Web. 16 Apr. 2015.

9. Donna Gordon Blankinship. "New Toilet Technology After 150 Years of Waste." *USA Today*. USA Today, 16 Aug. 2012. Web. 16 Apr. 2015.

INDEX

About the Author

Laura Perdew is an author and writing consultant. She writes fiction and nonfiction for children, including numerous titles for the education market. She is also the author of *Kids on the Move! Colorado*, a guide to traveling through Colorado with children. Laura lives and plays in Boulder with her husband and twin boys.